TAKE BACK CONTROL

WBW QUICK GUIDE

DARA GIRARD

CONTENTS

Introduction vii

TAKE BACK CONTROL

Disappointment 3
Discouragement 9
Doubt 29
Depression 37
The Ultimate Dream Killer 41
Comparison 51
Envy 55
Success 59

About the Author 67

Take Back Control: WBW Quick Guide

Copyright © 2006, 2021, 2023 Sadé Odubiyi

ISBN 13: 978-1949764697

Published by ILORI Press Books

Cover Design and Layout Copyright © 2023 ILORI Press Books

Cover design by ILORI Press Books

Cover Image Copyright © Lightsource/ depositphotos

All rights reserved. No part of this publication may be reproduced, stored in a retrieval system, or transmitted in any form or by any means, electronic, mechanical, recording or otherwise, without the prior written permission of the author.

DISCLAIMER

This book is not intended to provide professional advice and is sold with the understanding that the publisher and the author are not liable for the misconception or misuse of the information provided. The author and ILORI Press Books, LLC shall have neither liability nor responsibility to any person or entity with respect to any loss, damage, or injury caused or alleged to be caused directly or indirectly by the information provided in this book or the use of any products mentioned.

ILORI Press Books, LLC

PO Box #10332

Silver Spring, MD 20914

To writers everywhere who dare to live their dreams

INTRODUCTION

One of the greatest tools a writer of fiction needs is imagination. But while that deliciously handy tool can get you out of confusingly complex plot twists, shore up sagging middles and turn a simple assortment of different ideas into a sweeping multi-book saga, it can wreak havoc when paired with something else—emotions.

Fiction writers are paid to make others feel. That's our job. To make people worry, wonder, laugh, cry, shiver, smile. But if we can't get a hold of our own emotions, they can become the greatest barrier to our careers.

I've seen despair cause a writer to destroy their work. Envy cause another to spread lies about others and lose credibility.

Disappointment led to the demise of one author's promising career.

Over the many years I've been in this field, I've seen stories abandoned, relationships destroyed and dreams left to fade away. All because the authors couldn't handle the power of their emotions and what those emotions made them think and feel about themselves.

Feelings are like the imagination. They can be powerful, but they are not necessarily real. Feelings are not suitable indicators of anything being true. For example, just because you *feel* worthless or you *feel* down to your very core that your work is trash doesn't make it true. Just because you *feel* disappointed or discouraged doesn't mean that you're a talentless loser.

This quick guide, pulled from a major section of *The Writer Behind the Words*, is designed to give you focus. I hope by reading this guide you can to get to the heart of what may be standing in your way.

You have what it takes to be a success in this field. But don't be fooled. It takes skill. Not just the craft of writing but also by learning how to handle your thoughts and feelings.

If there's one thing I want to assure you, it is that feeling disappointed, discouraged, jealous, frustrated and other similar emotions is completely normal. You're human. These emotions are part of the journey and can make your fiction richer and more relatable. The key is to manage those emotions. Let them run wild in your stories. Let them burn, enlighten, destroy, empower your characters. But in real life? Don't let your imagination blow your emotions out of proportion and destroy the very thing you want: A happy, productive writing life.

It's possible. Let me show you how.

You have more power and control than you think.

TAKE BACK CONTROL

DISAPPOINTMENT

A fellow author, whom I'll call Patricia, recently faced a hard lesson in disappointment. She'd signed a second two-book contract with her publisher and had sent in her first book under the new contract. She was excited, and prepared her promotion schedule for the next year as she began working on her fourth book.

A few months later, she received notice that her editor did not like the third book and was reneging on the contract. She was let go without an explanation. No new book, no check—nothing. The disappointment was crushing. All her plans, all her excitement—dashed. Someone else may have crumbled, but Patricia didn't.

She continued to promote her first two published books and sent out queries on her third book. At a writer's conference she met an editor and convinced her to look at her manuscript. The editor agreed. Months later that editor offered Patricia a two-book contract. Another author, I'll call Marcus, found himself in a similar position but decided to choose the indie publishing route and his career is in high-gear.

A third author, let's call her Bonnie, indie published six books in two years. None of the books sold more than two hundred copies total. Did she call it quits? No. She kept writing and publishing, learning as much as she could along the way. It wasn't until her fifteenth book that she started gaining traction and an audience.

That is what resilience is about. Patricia could have let the disappointment stop her, but she didn't wallow in it. She shared her pain with fellow authors and kept sending out queries. Marcus looked around at other possible options and chose to publish his own work. Both writers wouldn't let one person's judgment stop them from their dreams and their readers are thankful. Bonnie kept improving her craft.

Disappointment sneaks up on you. Life is fine then WHAM! A book doesn't sell-through well, a story is pulled, an imprint closes or a magazine goes out of business before your article can get printed. It's okay to feel let down. It's okay to be upset, but move on.

STEPS TO DEALING WITH DISAPPOINTMENT

Share the disappointment like Patricia did. Don't keep your feelings bottled up, there's no need to feel ashamed. A setback is not a reflection of your self-worth or your talent. Another author had an editor reject her work because she liked "light, funny stories" and found the author's work "too dark."

TAKE BACK CONTROL

A setback is not a reflection of your self-worth or your talent.

I had an agent who lost complete faith in one of my books and refused to send it out. It was devastating, but I decided to part ways and move forward.

Keep sending out. Come up with a new strategy. Inventors face lots of disappointment. When an experiment doesn't work, they try a new way and keep on trying.

If you're in the mood, try to find a lesson in the disappointment. This is not the time for blame; think of it as a career autopsy. What went wrong? Patricia discovered her former publisher wasn't the right place for her work, Marcus learned that indie publishing better suited him. Instead of trying to convince the editor to change her mind (and likely stalling her career) both Patricia and Marcus moved on and found the right paths for them. Bonnie learned that there was a lot more skill—both in craft and product development—involved to grow and develop an international writing career.

HOW TO PERFORM A CAREER AUTOPSY

Take responsibility. If you signed a bad contract, followed certain advice that didn't work out ask why. Were you trusting someone else to take care of you? How might that have influenced things? What went wrong?

Analyze your decisions and the market. Were you trying to follow a trend? Is there a bad market climate? Were you marketing to the wrong audience? Is your productivity not what it could be? Are your products the best they could be? Are you expecting too much too soon?

Are you in the wrong writing field (fiction versus nonfiction)? Genre (mystery versus fantasy)? Many authors try to write what is popular and fail miserably because that is not their strength or interest. Also, what you like to read may not be your voice. I like to read dark mysteries, but my voice isn't dark enough. If I wanted to enter that field I would have to practice and make the effort.

Identify harmful habits. Do you miss deadlines? Make sloppy edits? Have slim plots or dull characters? Think your every word is golden? Refuse to practice? Procrastinate?

Are you using an old business model? In this digital age, trying to build a career similar to someone twenty years ago will hurt you. Many musicians have discovered that it's not about album sales but singles, merchandising, touring, etc... They won't wait for a major music label to build their career, but slowly build a fan base on their own. In the publishing industry many book and magazine publishers are not run as they have been in the past. Research them. If they are owned by a corporation, what does that mean for you and your copyright?

Also, if you are having a string of successes, such as receiving awards, having large sales, signing big contracts, etc... take the time to do a positive career autopsy. Too often people fall into success and don't know how to replicate it. Find out the 'why' behind your successes as well as your failures.

Your career is as long as you make it. Most long term career writers face two or more major career blowups, so you won't be alone. A bad year or more doesn't mean the demise or your career. A series of slow or no selling projects isn't the end. Don't make each book or story an "event" focus on building a body of work. That's what artists do. It's business as usual.

DISCOURAGEMENT

Discouragement comes in many forms. Rejections, poor reviews and the doom and gloom comments of a "Wet Blanket" can ruin a great day. It takes a lot of courage to face them and keep moving forward, but with the right knowledge you can.

REJECTION

> *I discovered that rejections are not altogether a bad thing. They teach a writer to rely on his own judgment and to say in his heart of hearts, 'To hell with you.'*
>
> SAUL BELLOW

First you feel as though you're dying. It doesn't matter how: whether you were shot through the heart, knifed through the gut, or poisoned. All you know is that your life will soon end and you don't care. You stand in front of your mailbox with your returned manuscript and a letter from the editor or you're staring at the one line response on your electronic device feeling completely alone in your grief and sense of failure.

Or worse you check your email, multiple times, and receive nothing. Not a word. You sent out your work and get nothing in return. Only silence.

Rejection hurts, whether it is a cold form letter or an encouraging "Try again." Rejections can make you begin to question yourself.

Who am I to write?
What the heck am I doing?
I'm an idiot to try this.
If I'm so great why doesn't anyone else think so?
"Don't take it personally" people say, but it feels personal.
I mean, the reply was addressed to me!
I put my work up but nobody's buying it. What am I doing wrong?

Rejections stinks. I know. I've received more than two hundred rejections in my career and still get some in the mail and online. However, it also means that I'm working, creating, and producing. Rejection is a part of life and definitely part of the writer's world. Don't give it power.

You reject things every day. You turn on the TV and flip through the channels. You stream movies and songs choosing one over the other. You go to a restaurant and skim through the menu until you see what you want. You go into the bookstore and pass hundreds of

books until you find one you think you will like. Why did you pass the others? Because they are unworthy or because they are poorly written? No. You passed them because you have distinct tastes. So do editors and readers. They are people just like you and me.

What does that mean? It means you're in the retail business and you have to convince people to buy a product. Not everyone will buy. Be ready to move on. It's part of the process. It stings, it burns, it wounds, but you'll heal. It's an opinion, not a life sentence. When an editor or agent says, "Doesn't fit our present needs" or "Not enthusiastic enough about this" they are not saying: "You are now sentenced to be unpublished for the rest of your life. Why are you trying to write? Why are you wasting my time? Quit now before you embarrass yourself and everyone who knows you." They are not laughing evilly as they toss your manuscript back to you. It's basically an "I'm not interested" and that's it. Keep writing; keep sending out if you want to be traditionally published. Or, if you are an indie publisher, you still have to keep on producing and improving your craft.

You never know what will make a sale. The fantastic story you wrote about life and death colliding may be turned down while your so-so article on ants infesting a picnic will get picked up.

> Rejection is a part of life and definitely part of the writer's world. Don't give it power.

It's not personal — it feels like it, but it's not. They don't even know you, and frankly they don't care. Editors have an agenda. Sometimes you're not on it; write anyway. Send out anyway. Keep publishing anyway.

> *I quickly learned that if I kept at it and plowed right through the rejections I would eventually get somebody to buy my wares.*
>
> ## CHARLES SCHWAB

Ah, but what about those nasty notes? The ones where the editor takes the time to tell you that you need writing classes, that you should stop writing and have more babies (advice given to Danielle Steel) or that your writing is "too slight" (told to Mary Higgins Clark). Be wary of such advice. Remember it's just an opinion. Unless there's a common thread in all your rejections, it doesn't mean anything. One editor will say they love your hero, but hate your plot; another will say they love your plot, but hate your hero. That criticism won't help you. So trust your gut. The publishing industry is a very subjective field. Only you know the value of your manuscript.

If you are going the traditional route, some editors are jaded readers cocooned in their own sensibilities and think in terms of salability rather than what readers will enjoy. They will reject a small town premise because they believe it will be uninteresting or because another book set in a small town didn't sell well and they think yours won't sell well either. They aren't bad people, just recognize that their job is to make money for their companies—magazines, small press, etc...— not to foster your writing dreams.

Your response to rejection will influence your career. If you try to avoid it, you could stop sending out or stay safe by sending to low paying markets. If you don't risk rejection, you won't have to face the lingering doubt that maybe you're not good enough. Unfortunately, however, you'll have made a career-killing decision, all on the basis of an overworked editor who has to make a split decision on whether she thinks you'll sell or not.

You will dislike this individual. You will wish that she break out in spots, lose all her teeth, and then one day see your book on the New York Times bestseller's list and cry bitter tears for having misjudged you. This is perfectly understandable. But let it go. Business is business. Don't threaten suicide or send foul letters. It won't change her mind and may influence others not to work with you. The publishing industry is small. Remember, editors have rejected wonderful works in the past and will continue to do so.

Readers will do the same. It's takes courage to try a new writer. Keep going, you'll get better and soon your audience will notice.

. . .

How to Recover from a Rejection

Remember what Barbara Kingsolver said: This manuscript of yours that has just come back from another editor is a precious package. Don't consider it rejected. Consider that you've addressed it 'To the editor who can appreciate my work' and it has simply come back stamped 'Not at this address'. If you want to be published by someone else, just keep looking for the right address.

- Use it as a reminder that you're working. Salespeople (no matter what field) expect to hear "No" because they know each "No" brings them closer to a "Yes." A rejection is not a brick wall, it's just a bump in the road. Keep moving forward.
- Picture yourself succeeding. Imagine rejection as a story you'll use in your acceptance speech as you're awarded a major prize.
- Have another market ready to ship out to right away so that you have hope again.
- Talk to a friend.
- Have a rejection party. Celebrate it. Buy a small cake or trinket so that rejection won't be something to dread.
- Reward yourself. Come up with a quota. If you get ten rejections, then you get to go to a movie. If you get twenty, you get to buy something you want. Have a trusted friend in

on the game and come up with a point system.
- Save them for your taxes. You can use them as proof that you are a writer.
- Read books about rejected authors who have succeeded.
- Recognize that sometimes the rejection is saving you from public humiliation. Your work may not be ready yet. Keep writing; keep working on your craft.
- Realize you're in a "taste" industry, rejection comes with the territory.

BAD REVIEWS

The lot of critics is to be remembered for what they failed to understand.

GEORGE MOORE

It's going to happen to you. Somebody with the intelligence of a pimple, somewhere is going to criticize your work; not constructively, mind you, but with the sole intent of demolishing your work and making themselves feel witty. You'll have to remember that the basis of wit is caustic comments. Wit is a game of words that should not be confused with wisdom.

Professional reviews are the bane of a writer's existence. Get a good one and you'll feel great and scared.

Get a bad one and you'll feel awful and scared. They are an unfortunate necessity but have no real guidelines. A writer must remember that reviewers have a motive — To be read and to keep their jobs. They want people to read them, not necessarily your book. They are writers with hidden agendas.

Some are kind; some are cruel. But they don't count, readers do. Stephen King and other top writers still get bad reviews and it hasn't hurt their careers (although undoubtedly their feelings were hurt). Stephanie Bond received a one star review in a major romance magazine for her book and that book ended up becoming one of her most popular books due to the one component the reviewer found so offensive.

Professional reviews must make way for the other end of the spectrum: reader reviews. They are all over the map. Some are insightful, some vicious.

That's okay. None of it is your business. Someone will like your work, others won't. Bland prose and safe writing rarely build long careers.

Hire someone to look at professional reviews to get pull-quotes. Otherwise keep writing. Read reviews if you must, otherwise ignore them and continue to create.

A good writer is not, per se, a good book critic. No more than a good drunk is automatically a good bartender.

JIM BISHOP

What do do With a Bad Review

My best advice is to never read reviews. Ever. But if you must...

- Remember that most people read reviews to find out about the book not the reviewer's opinion.
- Highlight the "money words" from professional reviews then use them in your marketing material. Some poor reviews have great quotes you can use.
- Review the reviewer. Is the review well written? Does it get the gist of your story right? Is it littered with personal attacks and unnecessary opinions? Angry readers blasted one reviewer in my local paper because her review of a non-fiction book was poorly done. She had misinterpreted the intention of the writer and misrepresented what the book was about. The paper had to apologize and the author got much needed publicity.
- Read the poor reviews of books you have enjoyed. It helps to put reviews into perspective.
- Flush it down the toilet or get your dog to pee on it.
- Cry with a friend.

- Find out what the reviewer disliked and then do that some more. That is what will make your work unique. Jean Cocteau said: Listen carefully to first criticisms of your work. Note just what it is about your work that the critics don't like — then cultivate it. That's the part of your work that's individual and worth keeping.
- **STOP READING THEM**

THE WET BLANKET

A successful man is one who can lay a firm foundation with the bricks that others throw at him.

DAVID BRINKLEY

Some people mistakenly believe that rejection and bad reviews are the ultimate discouragement. They are not. For writers (or any creative artist) the Wet Blanket is one of the most dangerous of all the discouragers because they mask themselves as friends.

As you pursue your dream, you will discover that not everyone will cheer for you. Some will give you reasons why you will fail. They will make statements like, "This is good, but it's no (fill in successful author's name)." "Twenty-five dollars for an article? You certainly couldn't live on that." "Do you know how competitive the market is?" "Hey I just saw that you got one star on Amazon.

Ouch! I'd hate to be you." "Another rejection? Man, maybe you should give up this writing thing."

They will tell you about how impossible it is to succeed as a writer. You must ignore them. Wet Blankets are usually blocked creatives or people who are fearful of change. Seeing you go after your dream may shine a light on the dreams they let die. Some will be relentless in their comments, you will have to distance yourself from them or end the acquaintance. With family members you can instruct them that they can talk about anything but your writing career. Set boundaries.

Also be careful of critique groups, workshops, and writing instructors. Great ones will inspire and encourage you and keep you moving forward. Bad ones can stop you forever. One writer stopped writing because a teacher read his story aloud in class then called it an example of how a story shouldn't be written. Another up-and-coming writer stopped her career because a boyfriend felt threatened by how much time her writing took away from him.

Group dynamics can create a group mentality. A teacher may only applaud a certain type of writing style and hold it up as an example for the other writers in the group to emulate. A critique group may belittle your story because it doesn't stay within the accepted structure of a certain genre. Don't let your creativity be stifled by someone else's limited vision.

Remember, there will be people who will not want to see you succeed. It's very important that you recognize these dream killers and stay away from them.

Dealing with a Wet Blanket

- Protect your joy. If you're excited about something, don't share it with someone you know won't be happy for you. Keep some secrets. Don't tell everyone what you're up to. Trust only a few with your dreams.
- Recognize them. Identify the Wet Blankets in your life and write a letter to them. You don't have to send it.
- Create a "no talk" topic. If you are with a Wet Blanket have a conversation limit.
- Remember the source. Unless they are living the life you want to lead or are sincerely invested in your success, their comments aren't helpful, useful or needed.
- Create distance. Change is difficult for many people. They would have a hard time if you lost weight or got a high paying job so let them deal with their feelings without dumping on you.
- Make new friends. Join groups or find another person who is a constant support and turn to him when the going gets tough.

KIDDERS

Next to Wet Blankets are Kidders. Those who make harsh comments then pretend to soften the blow by saying "Just kidding" or "Just joking."

- *This scene is so boring I could use it as a barbiturate. Just kidding!*
- *You didn't even go to college. How could you write anything someone would read? Just kidding!*
- *You really pump out those books like a true hack. Just joking!*
- *You write like a second grader. Just joking.*
- *You still write that crap? Just joking.*

The best way to combat these crude attacks on your ego is to:

- Not laugh. Many of us try to shrug it off and see the humor for fear of being deemed "too sensitive." Kidding is not funny. Don't laugh at what's not humorous and the person will get the message.
- Be careful who you share your dreams and good news with. Some people will not take the hint that their kidding is painful, so don't allow them to use you as a target.

- Realize that they're scared. A lot of humor comes from pain. It's their pain and you don't need to soothe it.

BAD EDITORS, AGENTS & OTHERS...

Because traditional publication depends so much on others, many writers put their lives in the hands of others and don't watch their careers. Don't do this.

In this new publishing environment I recommend you use a literary lawyer to review your contracts. Many current contracts have moved beyond the scope of most (not all) agents. Do your homework to make sure you're partnering with someone who has the legal background to handle the nuances of some of these complicated contracts. Also, even if you have a good agent, I recommend you request that your publisher do a split-payment so that you get your money directly instead of through your agent. There have been numerous cases of embezzlement where the writer ends up broke due to poor money management by their agent or agency.

If you have an agent, feel free to also have a lawyer review your contract. You're the one who has to deal with the outcome in the long term so pay the flat fee and get knowledgeable advice.

Not everyone has your best interests in mind. This field is crawling with scam artists. Your best defense is to make all your business relationships peer relationships or partnerships, rather than parent/child relationships.

No matter what stage you are in your career – you're in control. You have the last say. You are worthy of respect. If your assistant keeps missing deadlines, find another. If your accountant won't listen to you, find another. If you're afraid of your editor, find another. But taking abuse from the people you work with is unacceptable.

> No matter what stage you are in your career--you're in control.

How to Spot a Bad Relationship

- The person doesn't communicate. Doesn't return phone calls, messages, emails...
- The person makes you feel insignificant. Continually reminds you that you're not her only author.
- The person tries to change your writing style.
- The person puts you down. This can be by comparing you to others, belittling your work, where you are in your career etc...
- The person dismisses your concerns and says "trust me."

What to do When You're Discouraged

Clean out the clutter. Get rid of clothes you don't wear anymore, remove plates or pots you never use, toss out socks with holes or shoes that have no soles. Wear clothing that makes you feel good; use items that make you feel proud.

- Exercise.
- Get a hug. Sounds silly, but touch really can help. If you can get more than a hug, great. (Come on, don't be a prude).

- Watch a movie (preferably a comedy).
- Read about successful artists and what they did to overcome setbacks.
- Try something new. Fire your editor, switch publishing houses or magazines. Write in a different style and submit it to new markets.
- Do what YOU want to do. Celebrate the freedom to choose.

EXTRA

How to Get Rid Of a Bad Mood

Natalie had had a dreadful day. She'd received three rejections for the same story, gotten an email from her editor saying that they wanted a second rewrite, her computer had crashed and her husband wouldn't be home to help with dinner. She had two options: allow the day to make her miserable or work through her mood. She decided to get rid of her bad mood. You can too. Here's how.

- Take a deep breath and, while doing so, tense all your muscles. Hold for a few seconds then release while visualizing all the frustration, annoyance, and anger leaving your body. Now imagine yourself in a place of peace, whether it is in the woods or a jungle. Picture a gentle rain falling, washing

all your disappointments and frustrations away.
- Remember that the subconscious doesn't differentiate between what is real and what is "made up." Give yourself permission to daydream.

DOUBT

In the hours of adversity be not without hope
For crystal rain falls from black clouds

PERSIAN POEM

Doubt is a thief that often makes us fear to tread where we might have won.

WILLIAM SHAKESPEARE

Paul checked his mailbox and halted at the sight of the manila envelope with his handwriting scribbled on it. He tossed it on the table and did not open it. He was tired of rejections. After four years of trying and a drawer full of rejections, he was seriously considering giving up. How much battering could an ego take? It seemed no one but his family liked his writing and even they weren't sure anymore about his ability.

He'd submitted stories to literary magazines, trade journals, even publishing houses and all he'd gotten were form rejections with a "try again" here and there. He started to believe he was no good, that his dream would never come true. He knew he could never write like the best-selling author X. Unfortunately, he also couldn't write in the current popular style that seemed to make new authors rich. Nobody cared whether he wrote again anyway. He was ready to quit.

Months later, Paul finally opened the envelope and inside was a letter from the editor, enthusiastic about his work but asking for a minor revision in order to publish the work. Paul's heart fell. Because of his doubts, he'd lost a great opportunity.

Many new writers let doubt stop them. The "So What?" question echoes. If I stop writing, so what? No one will miss it. No one is waiting for my story or article. I don't count. Yes, you do. Many writers live with doubt. They write thinking that they have no talent, no gift, no skill but they continue to write. Keep writing. Each draft makes you better. Recognize the days before publication as an apprenticeship. You're in training like a musician or a dancer. Even if you have published a few books that haven't done well in the market, consider yourself in training at an advanced level.

If you're putting your work up for free and getting no

traction, realize that you may not be reaching your audience. This is where you have to think like a marketer—would you sell fish in the produce section? Would you post your literary work on a site that's targeted to teenagers? Writing is not a popularity contest no matter what the greater world tells you. There are many successful writers you've never heard of who have a loyal readership waiting for them, but it took time.

The time it takes to reach a goal can lead to doubts. But most people have doubts; having doubts is normal. After writing over 100 books and selling hundreds of millions of copies, author Nora Roberts/JD Robb, still worries when she sends a manuscript to her editor. If she still has doubts, you can too.

Steps to Handling Doubts

- Read about other writers.
- Repeat an affirmation.
- Read something you wrote that made you proud.
- Write your own happy ending.
- Take the initiative. Write and produce that play, post your stories, help promote a fundraiser, use your gifts to help others and your doubts will slowly fade.
- Recognize that not everything you write will reach a wide audience. That poem that cheered up a friend accomplished its

purpose. The article that informed your neighbor of the benefits of mulch finished its cycle.
- Offer your services for a fee. You never know, someone may pay you double what you expect if you ask for it. Give it a try. You may surprise yourself.

Doubt doesn't mean you don't have confidence. Doubt is normal. We all experience it, but you need to replace it with moments of joy.

EFFORT

What is written without effort is read without pleasure.

SAMUEL JOHNSON

Most people don't like the word effort. That is why "fast and easy" are always used to market things. Many new writers think that writing should be effortless. It should just flow from the mind to the paper. They think desire and talent are all that's needed for a successful career. Desire and talent fill up MFA programs all over the place, yet most of those hopefuls will never build a career.

Effort does not mean drudgery or suffering. When I looked at the dictionary I saw this definition:

noun

A vigorous or determined attempt

Attempt.

verb *Make an effort to achieve or complete (something, typically a difficult task or action)*

The act of writing isn't difficult. Being a writer—internally driven, committed, trusting your creative subconscious self is. In order to build and sustain a career you need to do this on a continual basis.

Some will not build their careers because they refuse to learn grammar, to write and read a lot; others will not grow their careers because they expect it to be easy. Desire and talent are great nouns, but to survive in this business you need verbs. Attempt is what will separate you from the pack.

Expect slow days, grumpiness, frustration, and fear, but continue to make the effort. New writers usually disappear at the stage where an editor suggests a change, or a rejection comes in, or a story isn't working or sales are low. They throw up their hands, believing others have it easier. Some do, some don't. Don't worry about anyone else, focus on you. Keep in the game and you'll reap your own rewards. Doubt hums a haunting tune even to the most prolific, successful writers, so realize that it's good. It means you want to do a good job and are striving for excellence.

> Desire and talent are great nouns, but to survive in this business you need verbs.

NOW!

Suffering is caused by wanting things to be otherwise.

STEPHEN LEVINE

In order to hear your calling and answer it, you must generously give yourself the gift of time. It's not how fast you make your dreams come true, but how steadily you pursue it.

SARAH BAN BREATHNACH

Someone's going to reach a treasured goal or seize a longed for dream before you do and it's going to hurt. Let me give you an example. Two teenagers sign recording contracts. One becomes a household name by nineteen; the other struggles and doesn't become known until he is thirty-four. You know these musicians as Prince and Michael Bolton.

It's not a race. It feels like it is, and in our competitive world you'll be told that it is, but it isn't. Whether you reach your dream at twelve or sixty-two the joy is just as sweet (sometimes sweeter).

Try to see writing as a race that never finishes. Remember it is a mission not a goal. One year a certain writer will get his first book or article published to great acclaim. For someone else it may happen months or years down the road. Take your time, it will come, your name will be seen by those who are meant to support you. It's hard wanting validation now, now, now! You want to write faster, sell more, be rich and be famous. NOW! Enjoy the process. It's the only thing you have complete control over. Wanting things now gives others power and then critiques will hurt more and rejections may be fatal. Keep going.

Another danger of being in a hurry is that scheming marketers, scammers and other parasites will use that urgency against you. No, a couple of sales does not mean you're now the best writer in the world. No, slow sales doesn't mean you're the worst writer in the world.

Being a professional writer takes time and never confuse making a living with building a career. Many new writers make a living for three to five years and then disappear. Just because you can easily put your work out on the marketplace doesn't mean that fame and fortune are just around the corner. Be careful of people who tell you otherwise, most have something to sell you. Focus on your long term goals, continue to study and grow.

DEPRESSION

David is a writer of short stories and articles, but can find no joy in his achievements. He is in a dark place. "I can't write," he says. "I'm always tired. I hate the morning. I sleep all the time, I can't think. I have no energy or ideas and nothing matters to me anymore."

Maya is a novelist. For the past five years she's written and published non-stop, but slowly the joy has slipped away. Now she cries all the time. Writing feels like torture. She's angry, disgusted with herself. Nothing gives her pleasure anymore.

When sadness turns into something deeper or darker, please seek professional help. The problem may be bigger than you realize and more serious than you can deal with alone. But if you're experiencing a mild case of the blues, it may be a signal that you need time off. Time to be alone and let your spirit rest. Many writers turn to stimulants to get them through: caffeine, alcohol, food or drugs. At first these choices may seem like a nice quick fix, but in the long run, some of these choices have ruined careers and lives.

If You're Feeling the Blahs Try This

- Hide. It's okay to not want to talk to anyone. To spend all day in bed. Pull the curtains because you hate the sight of the sunny day; unplug the phone. Eat what you want to. Read, listen to music, or cry.
- Get a friend to help you with the tasks you're too tired to manage, such as mowing the lawn, washing your hair, washing the dishes or ironing your clothes.
- Staying in a cluttered environment or feeling ugly can compound your depression, so have someone help you clean up. If the lethargy slips into the next day or into a week, please schedule time with a trusted friend or a counselor. It may be something more than the blahs.
- Schedule some down time every week. If you have a habit of feeling down, you may be pushing yourself too hard.
- Daydream about how things will be when you're past this moment.
- Get out.
- Talk to someone.
- You may be facing "burnout" and need to recover. Give yourself time.

WHEN IT HURTS TOO MUCH

Suicide is a frightening reality in this field. Being a writer is a solitary endeavor, and it can be painful. Being a fictional writer is about emotional honesty—some handle it better than others. Writing is one of the most overcrowded arts and you will get little respect. In no other field are beginners expected to be giant successes after the first try.

If you were a new doctor, no one would expect you to become an internationally known specialist after a year of practice. But publish one book, and people will ask you why you didn't make The New York Times Bestseller List, sell movie rights, get a $100,000 advance like the teenager they read about or earn close to a million like the stay at home mom who only started indie publishing a year ago. Ignore them. Guard your joy. If people ask you how much money you make, ask them their salary first then tell them if they're close. Or don't respond at all.

It's okay to be a beginner. It's okay not to make six figures with your first book (or sixth book), or a thousand dollars for your first article. You are on your way.

But if the pain lingers don't be too afraid or proud to seek professional help.

THE ULTIMATE DREAM KILLER

Everything you need you already have. You are complete right now, you are a whole, total person not an apprentice person on the way to some place else. Your completeness must be understood by you and experienced in your thoughts as your own personal reality.

WAYNE DYER

Argue for your limitations, and sure enough they're yours.

RICHARD BACH

> Excuses are one of the biggest dream killers in a writer's life.

Excuses are one of the biggest dream killers in a writer's life. Something happens and you're knocked flat. Excuses give you a great reason to stay down and never get up again. They are prevalent and insidious, causing a lot of untold stories and ideas to remain so. Why? Because everyone believes them.

I can't write because…

I don't have time.

I'm too old or too young or too hip or not hip enough.

I was awful in English or never went to college.

I don't think I'm good enough.

I have an illness and that makes me tired all the time or I can't see clearly or my arthritis acts up.

There are many excuses, but I'll address the three most common.

I DON'T HAVE TIME

Sure you do. You're just not spending it on your dreams. Like money, time is something you spend and many people waste hours. They say they'll wait until their kids are grown, or until they have a better job or until an extra hour is added to each day. The reality is that time will always be taken from you, if you don't know how to steal it. When I was going to college, working full-time and shuttling my mother to and from different doctor appointments, I would write in the waiting rooms, during my lunch break or on the metro. Another writer strapped for time hired a babysitter, another talked into a recorder while driving to work. Learn to seize sixty minutes out of every few hours or sixty seconds out of every couple of minutes. Become a crafty thief of time. Time is not money. It is a resource. You use it to build relationships, create products, learn, rejuvenate, explore, experiment and more. Learn to use it wisely.

How to Steal Time

- Make a list of what you do each day. Discover where your hours are really going. Find one activity that you can farm out or stop doing all together. For example, how many shows must you see every day/week? Can one wait until a later date? Do you commute by bus, metro, or carpool? Write on the way to work or on your lunch break. If you don't take lunch breaks, start.
- Use a recorder in the car, while cooking, folding clothes, walking.
- Go to sleep a half hour later or wake up a half hour earlier to write.
- Write in five to fifteen minute intervals. Just to jot down an idea. In the kitchen, while boiling water, scribble down a sentence: On Sunday, Malcolm discovered the body. Good

you're done for the day. Tomorrow you'll add something more and the day after that even more. It doesn't matter how much you put down, just that you write something. It's like using drops of water to fill a bucket. Eventually, each drop will accumulate into a story. Slowly you'll eke out more time to write.
- Put it in your schedule like an appointment. From this time to that I write. Make it an important priority.

Don't let time be the enemy of your dreams. Don't dream of the day when you'll have all the time you need to write. Make time now.

I'M NOT SMART ENOUGH

Life is my college. May I graduate well and earn some honors!

LOUISA MAY ALCOTT

You are smart enough and don't let anyone tell you otherwise. I doubt my fourth grade teacher would believe I'm a writer now. I missed most of recess that year because I was kept inside to redo my English tests (grammar, spelling etc.), but I still wrote stories and poems and plays. I kept writing. Successful or smart people recognize their limitations and hire others to compensate for them. You have all the skills you need to make your writing dreams come true and one of those skills is delegation.

Use other people's strengths to your advantage. Are you unsure about your subject? Talk to an expert. Grammar not a strong point? Read a book, hire someone, or get a trusted friend to look it over for you. Are you a poor speller? So what. Write the way you think the words are spelled then look them up later or just use spell check on your computer or have someone proofread. The one thing you need to remember is that readers want others to instruct them or to tell them a good story. They don't care about your limitations or shortcoming as long as your words do their job. You're only limited by your fears.

I HAVE A DISEASE/DISADVANTAGE

I will in no way belittle the burdens of a disease, but don't let it stop you. The writer Christy Brown (the subject of the movie *My Left Foot*, a great inspirational movie) had a major handicap and still made his literary contribution. Debbie Macomber overcame dyslexia to become a New York Times Bestselling writer. The late Eva Rutland was blind and used speech recognition. After his near fatal accident, Stephen King continued to write through the pain. There are authors who have continued writing after surviving cancer, struggling with muscular dystrophy, dealing with diabetes, migraines and coping with many other ailments.

I, too, struggle with a chronic illness that impacts my "quality of life." I faced ten years of being undiagnosed (and at times, misdiagnosed) and I continue to struggle in managing my illness, but my writing kept me going and continues to do so. I don't focus on my illness and I encourage others to do the same. Your words are needed.

It's the act of movement that differentiates the winners from the losers. Winners keep moving like the turtle, unlike the hare that finds reasons to stop. Get moving. Toss away excuses, they have no place in your career plan.

Excuses are easy to fall into and are the enemy of resilience. When you have written only three pages of a three hundred-page novel, the "I don't have time" excuse will pop up. A rejection turns into an "I'm not smart enough" campaign. You see a fresh-faced young writer get a million-dollar contract and you tell yourself that you could have written that book if you weren't always so sick.

Excuses are the perfect shield for fear and the longest and most painful road to regret. You can be yourself (flawed, imperfect) and succeed. Get rid of excuses and take responsibility for your dreams.

I know this section might make some of you angry. Many aspiring writers write me and say, "You don't understand! I have a really good reason!"

Okay, you caught me. Let me briefly discuss the

difference between a reason and an excuse. A reason has a solution after some thought, an excuse is never ending. Here's an example. Let's say a writer is always missing deadlines. Someone suggests she puts an alert on her phone as a countdown. She says she doesn't know how. Another person says they'll set it up for her. She says she doesn't like countdowns because they make her nervous. A third person suggests she make her deadlines sooner than she thinks so that when she misses it she'll still be ahead of schedule. She says...

Well, her reason has become an excuse. The first suggestion was fine. She could have tried it or something else, but the moment she found a reason why not she slipped into excuses. Excuses are always true. They're real and powerful and you will get sympathy. But use them at your peril. Most excuses are not good enough to combat regret.

After excuses, the next dream killer is the Poverty Complex. Many people think that writers are either very rich or very poor. But there are plenty of writers who are making a good living and you can be one of them. Don't fall into the Poverty Complex. Here are a few tips on how to avoid it.

MAKE MONEY MATTER

Because the thought of poverty is a dream killer, think of riches. Yes, there are people who will write for free. Don't worry about it. Set your standards and go for high markets. Choose clients and customers who will pay you.

Make sure to work with those who value your skill and will pay for it. Kill the starving artist stereotype. Unless it gives you pleasure, pay no mind to the statement "It's impossible to make a living as a writer." It's a poverty trap. People won't pay for writing if they can get away with it. But don't let them.

As a professional, demand to be paid. If it's a low paying market, make sure you're in it for the right reasons (good exposure, to get clips etc.) but don't stay there. Branch out into bigger markets.

Make money matter. You don't want to live on noodles for the rest of your life and you don't have to. You don't need to be greedy or obnoxious, just business savvy. A check or direct deposit always helps the ego.

Develop the key attitude that you deserve to make a living as a writer: Whether that is through self publishing, charging $100 an hour or demanding a high advance. Don't fall into the starving artist trap. The world at large will trick you into thinking that you must love what you do at the expense of money. But you have to eat. A person who hands out fries gets paid and so should you.

Book publishers don't make most of their money on books, they make it on selling the rights to those books. You're licensing content that can become much more. Synergy is the name of the game: learn how can you take one idea and transform it into different forms.

Licensure is where the money is. Educate yourself. How many ways can you slice the copyright pie? Audio, scripts, articles, merchandise, try to see the bigger picture before you hand over all your rights (please never do this).

Be strategic. If you decide to take a low advance or for a small market because there are other benefits to the deal, that's strategy. Taking a low advance or low pay because you're grateful someone's willing to pay you, that's a poverty trap.

COMPARISON

I will not reason and compare. My business is to create.

BLAKE

If you want to kill your confidence faster than a hasty rejection, bad review or degrading critique, compare yourself to others. It doesn't matter if the writer to whom you compare yourself is good or bad, you'll still feel miserable. Why? Because if the writer is bad you'll wonder why they're a bigger success than you are (published, better paid, better looking or, Gasp! younger). If they're good, you'll know why and wonder if you should even attempt to foist your inferior product on the unsuspecting masses. So stop!

Comparison is as useful an activity as pulling out your own teeth. It's painful and you'll look bad. Write, write, write!

> Comparison is as useful an activity as pulling out your own teeth.

Keep those blinders on. You're supposed to write because you have something to share and it will be unique because of your voice, your style, and your perceptions. There are no original stories or ideas, just original ways to tell them.

If you're feeling extremely down, take a hiatus from trade magazines. They applaud the chosen few and perpetuate the scarcity mindset, and you'll hate yourself for not being one of the chosen few. Fortunately, you're above that. There is plenty of praise to go around. Comparing will cause you to forget that you are lucky to be a writer. Many others dream to be, but just don't have the courage and they're miserable comparing themselves to YOU.

INTEGRITY

There's a lot of literary prostitution in the arts. Many writers sell their wares only for the money. I'm not against the practice, I've seen it make people rich, but I've also seen it destroy souls.

If you can keep one thing, keep your integrity. Always do your best. Don't be seduced into changing your voice or your style for money. This is not obstinacy, this is preservation. You must find the editor who gets your voice, because some won't. You want to be proud of your work no matter how small. Some writers change articles or stories to suit an editor, then when the editor still hates the work the writer is left with a dead piece.

People read to be entertained or informed. Do your best to meet those needs.

If you want to freelance, choose an area that you know about or that interests you. Who cares if at the time health writers are making a killing? If you know a lot about gardening, then this is a lucrative field for you. Become the best at what you do.

Genre fiction make you cringe? Then don't write it! Don't let the marketplace dictate your work. Write only what you can write. That's the path to success and brilliance.

ENVY

Of course, there will be times when you just can't help yourself and you will compare. That's when it will strike: A festering disease of the spirit. You'll feel embarrassed and disgusted with yourself and with the person who has made you feel this way (basically yourself, again). Envy. It's perfectly normal. Don't ignore it. Own your emotions; ignoring them will only make you feel worse. I hate it when someone suffers a particularly bad blow (fired, dumped, hurt) and her (purported) friend pats her on the back and coos a silly platitude. "Sorry your dreams are now in ashes, love. Don't feel bad." What the #@$!? What planet do you live on? I feel awful! Angry, pissed and plenty of other things. We are writers after all, and our ranting can be long and fierce. But that's what writers do for a living — feel. We feel everything, intensely, so when envy creeps up on us or grabs us in a chokehold, it lingers and rages. See it, feel it. However, some writers invite it to dinner and allow it to destroy their lives. I don't recommend that.

How to Handle Envy

- Write a story of someone envying you.
- Sulk for a day (it's allowed).
- Give praise. You don't have to be sincere.
- Admit it. If someone tells you about their good fortune say "I'm so envious," but realize that's not their fault.
- Give gifts (making someone else feel better can help make you feel better. You won't feel like such a jerk).
- Have a tantrum. No one needs to see.
- Read about top authors envying each other.
- Remember when you succeeded at something and treasure that time.
- Buy yourself something.
- Get writing so that you can write something that will have people envying you.
- Count your blessings and move on.

Sometimes envy sheds a light on what we want.

Sometimes envy sheds a light on what we want. Annoyed with the actor who has written a children's book? Write one yourself.

If you envy someone for being younger, prettier, taller or anything else you can't possibly achieve, write about it. Make a spoof of it. You may as well use your emotions for your art.

Still steaming because someone has what you want? Here's a little tale to help you. Remember being a kid and seeing the ice cream truck come around the corner? You try to rush to the front of the line so that your order will be first, but another kid gets there first. Before you lunge for the kid's throat, a wise guardian gently holds you back and says, "Wait your turn." Do that.

SUCCESS

If your success is not on your own terms, if it looks good to the world, but does not feel good in your heart, it is not success at all.

ANNA QUINDLEN

We all work towards success, yet most people don't know how to handle the onslaught of good fortune when it comes. The sudden adulation, money, and status can become another stress for which one may be unprepared.

Suddenly, you're no longer a person writing in solitude, you're besieged by a public that feels that they now own you. You will be subject to criticisms, spoofs, and gossip. People will demand more work, time and energy from you. If you're not careful, you may burn out. So you need to be aware of the hazards of success:

> You need to be aware of the hazards of success.

- Lost time. People will want you. They will request that you give speeches, interviews, and workshops. They will ask that you participate in fundraisers, judge contests or teach.
- Your phone will start ringing with a regularity you never thought possible.
- If you reach a bestseller list, you will be pressured to stay on the list or hit a higher slot.
- Your objectivity could change. Some writers who reach success start to believe their press and soon they become crazy with the belief that they are the "next best thing" and turn into a giant ego.
- Your core values may be influenced. Thought you'd never become a diva? When you have people hanging on your every word and have loads of disposable income it may be easy to arrive late to dinners or talk about yourself at every occasion.
- Friends or family members may become jealous of you.
- Family members or friends may accuse you of using them as characters in your work.
- You may overspend and find yourself in financial difficulties.
- Other writers may accuse you of stealing their ideas.

- You may have to travel to twenty-one cities in two weeks.

But you don't have to be a victim of success. All you need to do is learn to manage it in whatever form it comes to you.

Ways to Handle Success

- Take a break and reflect. It's okay to go on a vacation right after a book makes a big splash or after an article causes a huge controversy.
- Know your allies. You will likely lose some friends who will be envious of your success, but treasure those who stick by you and be aware that you will make new ones.
- Remember your mission statement. It is easy to get caught up in what others believe is "being a success." Whether that is partying, traveling, interviewing or the like.
- Mind your tongue. Don't put down those who haven't reached your level. It always amazes me how many published authors become snobs against the unpublished.
- Get an unlisted number. If too many people are calling you, don't be readily available.
- Learn to say "no." Many people will want your time, and initially you will want to please them all. You can't, so don't try.

- Hire help. Get someone to handle your correspondence or someone to help you with household chores. Hire an assistant to help you with the details.
- Meet others in the field to talk about strategies and tactics for handling success.
- Prepare for it. What would you do if you got $50,000-$100,000 in a lump sum? Would your bank accept it?
- Get a good, trustworthy and reputable person to help you manage your business (i.e. CPA, lawyer etc...) Many writers are not good business people and lose money quickly. Unless you have a trusted friend or family member who is good in business, do your research and hire someone who can help you with taxes, contracts, and other business and financial matters. You don't want the government or a lawsuit at your door. Also read and learn as much as you can because it's your career and no one else's.
- Study how success can hurt a business and come up with strategies to handle it before hand.

> Remember that success is not a destination; so be gracious when you pass it by. You'll always want more.

Your success may take time away from your family. In that instance, have a discussion with them so that everyone can learn to adjust to your newfound popularity.

Remember that success is not a destination; so be gracious when you pass it by. You'll always want more. One bestseller will lead to the desire for a second bestseller. One huge check will create the desire for a larger check. Keep your goals and mission in order. Don't let the thrill of success become a drug.

ABOUT THE AUTHOR

Dara Girard is an award-winning, national bestselling author of more than forty books.

She has written numerous articles for *Byline* magazine, *The Writer's Notebook*, *Romance Writers Report*, newsletters and e-zines. She has also interviewed many industry professionals on the Novelist Inc blog.

Visit her website at www.daragirard.com.

You can write her at:
   contactdara@daragirard.com

or

Dara Girard
   PO Box 10345
   Silver Spring, MD 20914

If you would like to receive a reply, please send a self-addressed, stamped envelope.

www.ingramcontent.com/pod-product-compliance
Lightning Source LLC
Chambersburg PA
CBHW062035120526
44592CB00036B/2164